First Light

Alex Chornyj

My name is Alex Chornyj, I am a reiki master teacher and as such my writing reflects the energy and light that surrounds my spirit. One who realizes their potential and purpose by developing their creative calling will be successful in their endeavour to reinvigorate the life force which is central to all of our spirits. I listen to my heart that speaks through my soul embracing the life within encapsulating the life without in a oneness leading to an inner peace. I am continually evolving physically, mentally, spiritually, emotionally and etherically in an upward ascendance towards a greater enlightenment. I have been published in The Canadian Federation Of Poetry, Poetry Super Highway, Touch Magazine in England, Decanto Magazine in England, Fashion For Collapse Magazine,I Speak Project, Awaken Consciousness Magazine, Earthborne Magazine, Gloom Cupboard Magazine,The Not Magazine, The Tower Journal, White Mountain Publications, and 2Sloitudes Magazine in Montreal as well as a host of others. I have been writing for approximately forty years and my inspiration is derived through my spirit guides. When I do public readings I often receive responses how my voice inflection carries a vibrational frequency that touches heart chakras in a soothing and calming manner. This binding of thoughts was manifested as a collaboration of an esoteric synthesis.

Contents

This book is dedicated to the healing of all life in our present pandemic crisis by the mantra. As the first light of dawn touches the earth, I heal all life on the earth completely.

Cleansing Rain

As light first touches
The dawn of a new day
Hope springs eternal
On the cusp of a mantra.
These words repeated
From a spiritual summit
To extend its influence
To encapsulate,
Then heal in its entirety
All life in a universal sphere
As upon this plane
Are those most vulnerable,
At or near a border
Has not yet called their names
But due to this nemesis
An early beckon is uttered.
Which is life in a nutshell
How fragile this can be
Taken before their time
Due to some infirmity.
Which is not necessary
Yet a wind none the less
Carries a contagion
Is indiscriminate in its path.
One's breath is shortened
By this such brevity
Has a smaller window
Through which to see.
A vanishing pane

A narrowing vision
A diminishing duration
To an illumination,
That dwells in one's eyes
Yet this ember remains
A hope with a cleansing rain
Earth and its inhabitants,
Can break free from its vice
Is like a tightening noose
To lift this burden
To breathe again unencumbered.

Sullen Star

It is not necessary
And unexpected
That one such as you
Would write such beautiful things,
As in these acts of kindness
Ardent words have
Touched my fragile heart
You did re-light,
A sullen star
As a dimness
Reclaims its former self
A shiny spot,
In the cosmos
Once more transmits
These reaching rays
Of everlasting brilliance.
By one awakened
Who by their own virtue
Cleared a dark opening
To reveal scintillations.
My eyes were closed so long
It took the warmth
From your essence
To revive me from,
A hibernation
In a sleeping stage
Once I felt this vibration
A smile returned to my soul.
I have you to thank

As you were the bridge
That let me cross
From one side to the other.
It was an expanse
With a deep chasm
That was in between
Now is invisible.
All because you took the time
In a sign of friendship
Did extend a hand
So let me find happiness again.

If The Walls Could Talk

I ended up back
Where I first began
Through three generations
Did this house change hands.
Here there are spirits
Mostly positive
Some who are not so
Get the good with the bad,
The yin with the yang
They all accept me
Which is neighbourly of them
To peacefully co-habitate.
If the walls could only talk
What would they say ?
From their perspective
This would be interesting.
The writing they could read from
The stories they would tell
Of all the goings on
Pitter patters of their feet.
Each with their own slant
An angle of origin
From experiences
They'd be able to speak.
As quite the history
Has passed in between
Lives that were lived
Ripples upon the waters.
At night I sit quiet

In the silence I listen
To that which transpires
Soft footsteps are all I hear.
When I'm into a good book
My cat is on my lap
At times I feel those claws
When she gets scared by sounds.
To me this is old hat
I'm waiting for words
That would be the cat's meow
Maybe as a person from their past life.

Binding Pages

I can see myself in you
This inner reflection
Has inter-changeable parts
Each as fine as the other.
I like to think
We're on the same level
I mean, it takes one look
To know this chemistry.
One which I relate to
I can call my own
But then there is
This one who mirrors mine.
At all times of the day
I come up with
The strangest things
To you they make perfect sense.
Were we born under the same moon ?
We share a glow
That has different shades
Whose shapes so identify with us.
I can start a sentence
Which only you can finish
I then punctuate
While you enunciate.
Together comes fluidity
A measure of consensus
I have your back covered
While your shadow,
Shimmers on my spine

A light ever present
Even when not near
This crescent is my shield.
As a silhouette
An invisible image
Embedded in my aura
Is the breath of your brush.
This breeze flows through
Etching in its wake
These lines of passages
Whose elements are our binding pages.

In Me – In You

In me you planted a seed
In me did this take root
In you have I gained faith
In you is this gate,
Through which I passed
As I stand where you are
I hear the birds singing
With these trees in blossom.
Their essence fills
With a sweetness
From your garden of treasures
Of infinite kindness.
In me is re-kindling
What is a lost art
In you are these steps
Which I now ascend.
As I near the summit
What comes into view
Are these timed shooting stars
Each with their own meaning.
A language which I grasp
As I'm at the edge
One after one
They encircle my third eye,
Then they embed themselves
Merging with my cosmology
Such an interaction
Enhances my comprehension.
In me is this sparkle

From your origins
In you is this savant
From whom I am elucidated.
In me is this woman
Who until you had not known
In you was this miracle
That would let me be my own person.
I think of what is possible
With you all can come true
For with each syllable
Your voice with its tones emboldens my shine.

Tender Years

Don't rush your tender years
You look in the mirror
Wanting to be older
But there will come a day,
When you wish the other way
Then it'll be too late
As the damage done by time
And the self-clogging,
Of your precious pores
Will bring on the
Early onset
Of white hair and wrinkles.
Your expanse that lies in front
Is far greater
Than the water
That's passed under your bridge.
Once this has reversed
The crystals in your hour glass
In declining numbers
Will lead to a curved spine.
Youth is a terrible
Gift to ever waste
The age of innocence
Is soon enough,
Replaced by reality
That is in stark contrast
To the fun filled approach
You so want to escape from.
Once you are out there

Your seconds accelerate
Seasons come and go
Like turning pages in a book.
Almost becoming a blur
One merges with another
Then your joints begin to ache
The advent of,
Your final chapter
So be happy how you are
Read to your heart's content
Run carefree in the wind while you can.

Point In Time

The earth has been talking
Only a few so hearing
You are one of them
With a direct line.
As you've been practising
What is dear to your heart
That near to your soul
This close proximity ,
Bodes well for your next step
Which comes with responsibility
To be a leader
With this new paradigm.
As an open channel
You have at times
Instinctively
Even unknowingly,
Been able to access
A knowledge that's invisible
Exposed due to your love
Through a firm commitment.
The old order
Has lost its usefulness
You are ready to assume
A position of merit.
Been long in this transition
But a shift of this magnitude
Requires a coordination
Whose adeptness is learned,
Through repetition

An untiring devotion
To a faith that's redeemed
Why you've gained entrance,
Through a concealed gate
As your eyes see beyond
Physical limitations
Here your purpose,
Will be realized
Why you came into this world
At a point in time
Of such immense change.

One Who Walks

Transparency
A far- fetched idea
That one with moral fibre
Can tell it like it is.
These ivory towers
Soon will be made with mud
Who in their right mind ?
Thinks they are better,
Than all the others
Proven to be contrary
As we are not little people
Who lack substance.
We deserve respect
To be told the truth
It's the same old story
Beating around the bush.
But we stand beside them
Not precariously below
It is eye to eye
Egalitarian,
Not in a hierarchy
Of have and have nots
As each life is precious
Each matters equally.
To be treated less
Or differently
Is more than a
Slap in the face,
This is tantamount

To a declaration
From those ethnocentric
Who lack the very criteria,
From a blinded consciousness
From a self-made pedestal
That crumbles in the face
Of an articulate inquiry.
He who makes himself
To be some form of deity
Pales in comparison
To one who walks the earth with the rest of us.

Deafening Count

This world catastrophe
Will re-define
What sacrifice means
To survive this calamity.
As the tighter the reins
Will lower the mortality rate
To let up too soon
Shall have a hefty price,
The cost of which
Will be the burden
On those left standing
As the sheer numbers,
Are staggering
The implications
Of seconds lost
Due to political differences.
When there's not a moment
Should let come to waste
As time is of the essence
To prevent a worsening,
Of current conditions
As it's actions, not words
That need attention to detail
To apply the brakes,
Not to fan the fire
Whose heat is approaching
The melting point
To a vanishing experience.
As this is a consuming wind

Akin to a black hole
Swallowing all in its path
Leaving devastation,
Behind in its wake
Tracks that are singed
Unrecognizable
At its bleakest,
For this is far from over
The worst is yet to appear
You'll know when it does
As the bell will toll a deafening count.

Shadow In A Line

The stains in the streets
The cries and the screams
From young to the old
Victims of anti-semitism.
To be caught in this vice
A sweeping net
Meant certain finality
An end to what we cherished.
That being family
The love between
The air that we breathed
The lives that we shared.
Snuffed out like a candle's wick
A flicker burning brightly
Then came this siren
Warning of impending disaster.
As all the lights went out
One after another
From those who went into hiding
Or ones found unawares.
With no second chances
As once you were there
Behind the iron fences
You fell into despair.
Stripped of your dignity
Right to the bone
Losing face with humanity
With the name you were born.
Branded with a number

To be catalogued
Only seen as
A shadow in a line.
An image of your former self
An identity stolen
Bereft of all hope
From walls of blackened soot.
A time in history
When even war
Was devoid of honour
Salvation came by passing to the next existence.

Tranquil Ripples

A new dawn arises
On a day with changes
Those with the ability
To adapt will survive.
This is a challenge
Unlike any other
In more ways than one
This is under,
A different sun
It doesn't seem
Even the same world
With an augmented vibration.
Old rules don't apply
When I look up
I peer into a sky
Whose origins,
Are beyond me
Not only foreign
From far in the distance
Could be galaxies,
That are in between
As these constellations
Are of a rhythm
Which are out of tune.
But this is the realm
In which we now
So find ourselves
We either adjust,
Or then succumb

To its idiosyncrasies
Until I find my way back
I will make the most,
Out of a bad situation
This river has rough waters
But it's within
Our human spirit,
To come out the other side
Where tranquil ripples
Barely make a fuss
It's getting there wherein lies this journey.

Extra Mile

We will get through this
Must stay the course
As losses should be kept
To an absolute minimum.
By leaning on each other
A burden is shared
A weight although arduous
Can be endured.
Unselfish tendencies
Are to be encouraged
When you see one struggling
Do what you would want,
In the same pinch
Then done for you
It's looking at
Two sides to one coin,
It is this empathy
Putting yourself
In another's shoes
So brings you to the doorstep,
Of a higher existence
As you put others first
Ahead of your own needs
This follows from insight.
As you go the extra mile
You come upon a field
That's within your vision
You plant these seeds,
Then with sun and water

You let hope spring eternal
From a kindness
That dwells deep in your heart.
We are of a reflection
A likeness that is our bond
As we give without
The expectation of return.
If anything
It's the corresponding smile
Which begins to emerge
That is our greatest reward.

False Bottoms

It matters not
What other people say
It's how you see yourself
This only counts.
You live your life
According to principles
Which guide you the person
Not how some wish you to be.
Each is master
Of their own destiny
Every moment is precious
You alone steer,
In which direction
Your ship is heading
These coordinates
Come by your calculations.
An independent mind
Relies on itself
To shape its future
Not on the whims of,
Such worthless peers
Who would do you wrong
Laughing at your misfortune
These are not friends.
And truth be told
Some must learn the hard way
From a school of sharp rocks
That in the end,
Knock some sense into them

After seeing those held
In such high esteem
Make a mockery,
Of a sacred trust
It is only then
When one's eyes really open
You see their colours.
Such is judgment day
When you turn the page
On false bottoms
Finding firm ground to stand on.

Day and Age

A good feel story
About a ninety-nine year old man
Retired from the British army
Who wanted to raise funds,
For the National Health Service
By doing laps
Around his garden
With a walker.
He started a page
With the intention
Such was the goal of
A thousand pounds,
He exceeded this by
A rather large margin
Like three million pounds
And still counting.
Says he has more in him
So around he goes
A wind in his sails
Has him breathing new life.
Wants to do his part
Beyond that fulfilled
Only getting warmed up
Such a sparkle,
In those dancing eyes
He supplies the motivation
Inspired by a motive
To help in any way possible.

In this day and age
It is remarkable
To come across
Such a purple heart.
Smiles from ear to ear
Knowing he makes a difference
That one person alone
Can bring hope to tomorrow.
In him is a passion
From whence a young lad
As long as he is here
This river's stream runneth pure.

Serenity

Now more than ever
I want to sit by a brook
Hear the gentle spilling
Of droplets descending.
By closing my eyes
I become one of them
Circling in pools
In search of serenity.
The bubbles are bursting
This popping sound
Reminds me of beginnings
In an ethereal forest.
As these surroundings
Are where I remember
My first cries came
Ushering me into this world.
As I've lived many lives
No two the exact same
Been aware, been taken
Always then given.
Chances to experience
Different sides
Of these are plenty
Each with its own purpose.
Now the earth is speaking
With an emphasis
On our origins
On why at this time.
Our paths so cross

The point to all of this
Is to awaken
From a slumber.
To placing the similar
With their equal number
To seeing the elements
As they truly exist.
Taking time to absorb
In their barest form
To first acknowledge
Then to live a life by its rhythm.

Maze Of Mists

You don't go with the flow
More like against the grain
Your mind has its own thoughts
Not borrowed or suggested.
You are self-made
Care not to be popular
But your decisions
Hang not from a pleasing thread.
Don't follow a trend
Have your trademark
This stamp of approval
Has, but one in its audience.
Once you make a move
Which is well conceived
You are not apt to change
With no return policy.
So you're stringent
Will not flip flop
Like a fish out of water
These eyes have permanency.
You look at all the angles
Listen only to yourself
Trust an inner intuition
That errs on the side of caution.
See beyond the obvious
Peer through the inconspicuous
In a maze of mists
Can interpret subtle signals.
Want to be thorough

Not near to partial
By full scrutiny
Have an appreciation,
For what lies in front
As there are pitfalls
Yet through conversion
You then extrapolate,
While others go beneath
Due to hastiness
You stay above
Due to a slow, but level head.

Lost Soul

At such a tender age
Of only fourteen
I came face to face
With my own mortality.
Working in my parent's store alone
Being the victim
Of an armed robbery
Having a gun,
Pointed at my forehead
With shock overwhelming
Pictures like a comic strip
Flipping by in silence.
As the mind was aware
Of the gravity
From the situation
A weight I found hard to bear.
To think I might die
When all of my dreams
Not yet even off the ground
At that time I was a lost soul.
This lasted for a minute
Of an eternity
Whichever came first
I felt helpless.
When the perpetrator
Fled from the premises
I called my sister
Then the hell began.
As she arrived

Out of breath running down the street
The police were given
My full description,
Of what the person was wearing
He had a nylon over his head
But I still looked at mug shots
At the station until,
The early morning hours
They caught up with him
Charged and found guilty
Yet my loss of innocence was the greatest crime.

Time In The Wind

When you come into this world
You are not empty handed
Have all the tools
Just need to learn,
How to use them
Responsibly
Each has their own set
Which compliments their abilities.
Some find out sooner
A few later on
Or never at all
Depends on their focus.
As priorities change
With time in the wind
What you are today
Is far from that you'll be,
Once you begin to ascend
As with maturation
Angles are altered
From how one views themselves,
In the wider picture
For a narrow scope
Widens its aperture
To accommodate,
This synthesis
As a loose knit
Tightens its circle
To become more defined.
As a mind early on

Is all over the map
To find its niche
Continuity must be found.
An inward shift
Zeroes in upon
A particular point
Small, yet poignant.
From this tiny sphere
So emanates
A strengthening beacon
Takes on a life of its own.

Pulse Of Emanations

The beauty of this
Is in its simplicity
Requiring nothing more than
The strength of one's,
Natural work ethic
By this alone
Are apt to succeed
To push through challenges.
It is the single aspect
Sees you rise above
All flood waters
Staying current,
Not being overwhelmed
Taking strides as they come
Going with, not against
The grain that is oneself.
In this direction
A flow is not abrasive
By means of friction
But transcends boundaries.
Life is full of these
It's what we do with them
How we respond
So gauges reactions.
The trick to minimizing
The degree of difficulty
Is to think, not complain
To advance your cause.
No one wishes

To go backwards
To be in reverse
Is contrary to our purpose.
There are many unknowns
Hiding in crevices
Or around some corner
So awareness is a good trait.
Not to go in blind
But constantly
Having your finger
On the pulse of emanations.

Living Colours

You find it within
To summon from a stream
In which so dwells
What glistens in the sun.
Reaches down to depths
Have only known darkness
You are the pathway
Through which this glow channels.
You bring out in mornings
A shine from the east
Like a pin to a magnet
Inner charisma has drawn.
The want from your will
Is a guiding force
You think, then envision
As such comes to pass.
In this manifestation
You cultivate
A barren field
Back to a fertile plain.
In you is a touch
That can't be explained
In its purest sense
Is a charmed existence.
So exemplify
The good in all people
In you, ones see reason
To once more believe.
Imagine that

Lead by example
Bring to the surface
What others can only dream of.
You put into words
These living colours
With you life comes alive
In an exuberance.
So you awaken
Parts in most kept dormant
You're like an eternal spring
From which flows this fountain of youth.

Resounding

So lit a candle
With a butterfly at the front
From a breathless nature
Crystals at the points,
This healing circle
With a picture of those
The center of this focus
To affect a convalescence.
A rhythmic melody
Of calming tones
In soft permeations
To loosen impediments.
Which have a hold
Don't want this to spread
Nip it in the bud
In a best case scenario.
This has the potential
To be detrimental
Want to avoid
The absolute worst.
Have to be disciplined
Surround entirely
In a smothering sweep
To rejuvenate.
So as this flicker
Adds to the mantra
This transcendent bridge
Connects this place,
To a distant spirit

This swirling vibration
Is resounding
In its intended spectrum.
Which is strongly felt
Any less would not suffice
But it's the continuity
Of repetitive beats,
So have their desired impact
To transfer negative energies
Into positive affirmations
That lift a colossal impairment.

Elucidating Axis

I see with my dreams
They are an extension
Of who I am
Writing the script,
To my story
As I've been in touch
With the other side
This view has an open window,
Through which does flow
These premonitions
Each has a message
Once I interpret,
I add to my mosaic
Each is a piece
A silver sliver
That dangles a thread,
Freely blowing in the wind
Each night comes a breeze
So ushers in
A new insight.
Which is pertinent
To the path I'm on
As these spaces slowly fill
More is revealed.
At times I ask why
What has been shown
In the end this reason
Bears a resemblance,
To this common theme

That time after time
By each revolution
I draw closer to my center.
My comprehension
Becomes more succinct
As my eyes recognize
With greater clarity,
What it is I'm supposed to know
Which guides my next step
On an evolving
Elucidating axis.

Pictographs

Picture yourself
In a different
Place and time than where
You are at present,
This can be in
The past or the future
Which one speaks to you ?
To such are you drawn ?
Or more inclined
As we all have moments
Of clairvoyancy
When our stars are aligned.
In their proper order
With the least amount
Of restrictive friction
Leaving us free to pursue.
Without constraints
A time of contentment
As dreams can come true
Just by creating this intent.
This fluid motion
Has no such gates
As your visibility
Is enhanced, not reduced.
There are no brick walls
You can will what exists
Prudent and proactive
In these altruistic visions.
A state of nirvana

Your own paradise
In peace and prosperity
In a world of virtue.
An untouched beauty
As life begins
Untainted, unblemished
In its purest form.
Such is this painting
So colours your soul
With auspicious aspirations
From pristine pictographs.

Phenomena

While out for a walk
I looked directly
At the warming sun
I saw an aura,
That surrounded this orb
With a rainbow
Around the edges
This was a rare occurrence.
It was only visible
With sunglasses on
By the pupils only
This appeared as a milky cloud.
Such a phenomena
Was meant to be seen
By those whose sight
Had become unveiled.
Who are at or near
This revealing threshold
As this circular entity
Is like a portal's entrance.
Ones devoid of fear
Pass through unimpeded
As from this doorway
Higher echelons,
So avail themselves
To be there at the moment
By a silent knocking
Only an intuition,
Would affect a cognizance

To fully expose
In all of its glory
This shining brilliance.
To be immersed
Within this cosmic sphere
Endows in its entirety
Evolving third eyes.
To cross over
To transcend a realm
From one thin space
Is a humbling experience.

Fanned The Flames

A summer beneath the trees
A heart stolen
By one with glittering eyes
Promised to be forever.
From opposite sides of the tracks
Two different worlds
But when one met the other
It was lights out.
Could not get enough
Wanted more crystals
In their hour glass
So hard to say good night.
Showed her the old house
Barren and drafty
She wanted in on the plans
A painting room that,
Overlooked the water
White outside with blue shutters
Then it all fell apart
She left to go to college,
He wrote her a letter
Every day for twelve months
Her mother hid each
She waited seven years.
But she heard nothing
So then moved on
He never lost hope
As his father gave him funds,
With which to buy

The fixer upper
He did to her wishes
Thinking when he finished,
Fate would lead her
Right back to him
Seeing an article
In the local paper,
About his restoration
Once more fanned the flames
Destiny so intervened
It was like time had stood still when he saw her again.

Near To Our Heart

The tunnels we pass through
The one we stay in
Which speaks to us
About who we are.
What we identify with
For when we settle down
It is in a place
That is near to our heart.
As the apple
Does not fall far from its tree
So stays in close proximity
To a pulse that beats within.
So instinctively know
Of the existence
Of a shared chemistry
Courses through our veins.
To where we are drawn
Is from first we so come
A circular orbit
Leads us back to peace.
As at times we may get lost
But this beacon inside
When we're off this path
Brings us to our compass.
That with patience finds
A certain rhythm
Is unique to the person
A particular resonation.
Once a recognition

Reveals a symmetry
This congruent flow
Puts two in alignment.
To become parallel
When side by side
A dawn from a horizon
Shines equally on both.
Pointing to a mark
To which each has
An affinity
With a common focus.

Caressing Waters

The outside is not always
Reflective of what's
On the inner
Layers can be deceptive,
Just like a mirage
For one reason
Or another
To suit a particular,
Time of the day
Or some facet
That may have an
Underlying hidden agenda.
It is never good to judge
As we all have
These imperfections
It's best to stay impartial.
Each image evolves
We are not what we were
Nor what we will be
In a constant state,
Of transformation
In a shifting
Flowing consciousness
With wave after wave,
Sands etch each stone
As do caressing waters
From these influences
Forming elements,
Have a hand in

Creating perceptions
Which each by its symbol
Is a tool of change.
In minute detail
In this metamorphosis
The slightest alteration
Can cause the emergence,
Of an angle
Through whose lengthening lens
Comes a moment
Of enlightened elucidation.

Angel

From my first breath
You have been so kind
Your words of encouragement
Have been the calm,
In all of my storms
As long as I can remember
A love like a mother's
Has been a joy in my heart.
You're here for me
No matter the reason
An unconditional caring
A tide that always returns.
As the moon is at night
Your glow has shone constant
To me has been a guide
Lighting a path,
To travel through my dreams
Your voice with its sparkle
In a positive sphere
Has enchanted my world.
To all who come in contact
You leave an impression
This indelible mark
That is a sign,
Of a serenity
From a peaceful dove
Who is forever
Within a tenderness.
You've gone the extra mile

Time and time again
Making a difference
Sharing a warmth.
These rays have stayed near
Like your gentle nature
In touch and in tune
With all that so shines.
You are like an angel
So has a happiness
Kept you endeared
To me you're an inspiration.

Good Of The Many

To look at life
In a different light
So begin to appreciate
Even the air we breathe.
Freedoms taken for granted
Now seen as a privilege
To be out and about
Or in the presence,
Of some anomaly
Which we either adapt to
Or suffer the consequences
Which can come at a higher price.
We choose the one
That is less severe
Pales in comparison
To that of indifference.
Can read the writing
That is on the wall
Don't let personal matters
Make issues worse.
For the good of the many
Far outweighs the needs of the few
We are all flesh and blood
Not some deity.
It's one thing to err
Only to affect ourselves
But when larger
Decisions are made,
They must consider

The welfare of the state
Or the province
Where the impact,
Will be experienced
It is irresponsible
To be short-sighted
Causing suffering to others.
A vision should
So encapsulate
All possibilities
To protect the most vulnerable.

What Lies In Front

It's never too late
To turn a page
To change a leaf
To start over.
We have many dimensions
So much to learn
About ourselves
For if I had three wishes,
One would be for
Peace throughout all universes
As there's more than
The one we're in.
I would then seek
An unconditional love
To spread its wings
Then ascend us to,
My third and final request
That each could realize
Their purpose within
To live this destined path.
To grasp with gentleness
To push through these walls
That hold us back
From reaching our potential.
As in life we're given
Such obstacles
In the same breath
The tools with which to use,
To one day overcome

This adversity
To find our inner light
Let it shine upon.
What has always been near
So close yet so far
Until we come to know
Who it is that we are.
When this day dawns
We come out from behind
With the knowledge in hand
To comprehend what lies in front.

Perpetual Motion

You live, you love, you laugh
So find the time
As precious as it is
To smell the roses,
From one day to the next
Can be here, then gone
Why you've adopted
A deep sense of gratitude.
You do not fear change
So respect the process
You reserve an invitation
Crosses all boundaries.
You do not take lightly
Fact why you are alive
None of this is by accident
You see the wisdom,
It does not escape
How you came to pass
You are of an energy
Which always exists.
You come by this honestly
As you are a seeker
Of an infinite truth
So absorb, then share.
For what is the good ?
If you keep it to yourself
This blocks a channel
To an eternal stream.
This flow is the key

For continuity
In the same breath
It is a privilege,
As equal responsibility
To further a cause
To bring to the surface
Not to be held asunder.
When you act in good faith
These tendencies
So grease the wheels
Of a perpetual motion.

Precious Moment

You walk where you will
You cry when you will
You smile as you will
You breathe with a love of life.
You think what you will
You do as you will
Free reign is your will
To be as an,
Unencumbered flowing breeze
That pushes high and low
So sings a melody
As it rushes through valleys.
You were born with
This unbridled aura
Has a sense of its own
You take each day,
With equal amounts
Of bitter and sweet
This way you balance
Not leaning to one side.
Straight down the middle
Is your favourite path
You learned long ago
So receive what you give.
Why this passion
Drives your ambitions
To reach as far
Even further than the eyes can see.
You touch as does a feather

Why you're remembered
Is due to an undying
Vigour that dwells within.
You care with a heart
Has a start with no end
Just goes on and on
Into infinity.
You live as you believe
Being here is a privilege
To savour each
Single precious moment.

Endowing Version

One night I had a dream
Of a distant shore
Could see the outline
Of a delicate face.
I heard a faint voice
One which as this proceeded
Became more distinct
As she called out to me.
I felt my spirit
Leave its shell behind
As I searched the origin
Of this fair maiden.
Upon her request
I found where she was
Alone and stranded
But why did she go ?
Outside of her world
Out into the cosmos
Said she felt a presence
A warmth from a far off star.
I answered because
This was beyond
My normal sphere
In which one appeared sincere.
I found her crying
A story for the ages
I was drawn in a way
To be her protector.

A chivalrous heart
She was in need of.
Was so dishonoured
I endeavoured to restore.
I gave her an angle
She had not seen
From my part of the universe
Came an endowing version.
An answer forthcoming
As I took her hand
Fit in mine like a glove
She offered her love in return.

Chrysalis

Just keep it together
The days pull you apart
From the constant pressures
But as you drift off,
Into deep slumber
There comes a synthesis
An integrating constellation
In a unifying theme.
That here amongst us
Lies the means to create
To tie up loose ends
To finish fragmentation.
No one likes slivers
Or empty saucers
But what's complete
In its full spectrum.
The shape of things to come
A world whose seams
Are no longer abrogated
But one intact length.
Imagine that
To once and for all
Be in a position
To weave with the wonder,
Of an unfrayed thread
Whose very stitches
Won't become unravelled
Under any condition,
To be a source of strength

To wield with compassion
Not reckless abandon
But a clear insight.
Which does not lose focus
Has a steady eye
In the midst of this all
In the center of calamity.
This then is integrity
A dawning influence
Wraps one in a chrysalis
To emerge as a brilliant dragonfly.

Enigmatic Waters

If there ever was a time
Now at the present
Is a motion afoot
To remove the blinds.
As the sun is at its peak
Gone is the ambiguous
In favour of the succinct
To peer through this mist.
One that's floated upon
These enigmatic waters
What seems like an eternity
Kept the masses,
Out of the loop
But the circle has expanded
As the watchers knew
It always would.
The moment in our history
Is at our doorstep
When a knock is heard
We are ready to listen.
As the other side
Is not for a select few
As they would have us believe
We have, but to answer.
The words forthcoming
Will mean we have to adapt to change
Which is an inherent
Part of our chemistry.
These signs and symbols

We assign meaning to
By an internal instinct
That interprets such language.
So we go inside
By entering we accept
These endowing vibrations
Which enhance our comprehension.
It's not as hard as we thought
As the pillars have long been in place
For by reading these etchings
We see ourselves in the images.

Opening Eyes

Where do I fit in ?
Not where I am
As I'm not content
With the status quo.
I have to be brave
This requires courage
To make a break
With the same old, same old.
I'm better than that
I see myself
In the distance
In an atmosphere.
That's more to my liking
This will take time
It's not all about me
But those in my circle.
I have my friends
They know who they are
I was away for awhile
I'm back with earnest.
Ones who are true to me
They accept my hand
With all of my faults
As we are all imperfect.
I want to be happy
I somehow lost track
Of what's important
Not a nice feeling.
My sights re-adjust

To a wider span
I was caught in a jam
Like icebergs on,
A northern river in spring
I came to my senses
One night when alone
When I heard the words,
From one with significance
Who saw what I could not
Now my heart is
In a better place thanks to my opening eyes.

Nature

The person is about their heart
What dwells inside
When the within shimmers
The exterior follows suit.
One's physical appearance
Is all well and good
To keep them healthy
But if the sole focus,
Is for the ego
Then this has shortcomings
In shallow waters
In the priorities,
Of a misguided fascination
As eyes that turn inward
Lose sight of what's important
For without the peripheral,
There comes distortion
In this visual field
Failing to recognize
Devoid of a sentient gaze.
What's truly significant
As there you scratch the surface
Always looking in a mirror
Searching for a,
Personal compliment
But when the glass cracks
Reality may set in
With the realization.
It's not the end all

As the looks fade in time
Whereas one's light
Is forever infinite.
When you find this truth
It is an awakening
A diving destiny
Aligns you with your dawn.
To be on a straight path
Not going in circles
To grasp with a sensitivity
The nature of this existence.

First Move

The wind in my sails
Is the impetus
Which drives my ambitions
Now more than ever before.
Don't rest on past laurels
Nothing ventured
Is nothing gained
As it's through interactions,
Where one learns to dream
But to put into force
One must apply themselves
Not sit back and wait.
As a couch potato
Is as the word describes
Not in my vocabulary
For by taking chances,
So make your own breaks
To have a door swing open
To even come ajar
Means you make the first move.
To instill life
You need to breathe
To see prana flow
Have to extricate blocked gates.
Then these channels
Can be slowly filled
With a sustaining essence
That pushes you along,
To stay in one place

You may become rigid
To have an active mind
Then use what you're born with.
I don't twiddle my thumbs
I get involved
I'm the reason behind
The source of my vigour.
I go to the center
Then out to the margins
So cover all the angles
As we reap what we sow.

Syllables

An underground aquifer
Bubbles emitting
Popping out of the earth
Starting its own,
Downhill flowing stream
So cool, sparkling clean
Pachamama creation
Of magical proportions.
A rare sighting
In this part of the world
Not known for such
Awe inspiring,
Natural occurrences
A liquid geyser
Playing these chords
From transcending melodies.
As from out of nowhere
Did these drops begin
To quietly appear
In synchronistic syllables.
To be a sustenance
For a thirsty forest
Trees ever grateful
For life's pure radiance.
To place our fingers
Within this pool
They swiftly vanish
Inside of this tunnel.

As the sediment here
Is not solid
Of a looseness
To permit this release.
One of the true wonders
Born from pressure beneath
Seeking an upward path
Through parallel striations.
From these pushing chutes
Form gurgling channels
Once at the surface
They skim across in constant beads.

Caressing Calm

Between us was this hedge
As I peered over
I did so because
I heard this angelic voice,
Like from another world
Where upon floating mists
Of rainbow hues
Welcome wispy fairies.
For on her side
Ran an emerald stream
Reflecting in the night sky
As does a northern borealis.
Swirling to and fro
In which I lose myself
Letting my spirit be levitated
In an air of auric articulation.
To be as if I had wings
A softness in the breath
Whose inhalations
Share a gentleness.
As I saw an opening
I let my arm enter
No sooner had I
Than a warmness,
So touched my hand
The suddenness
Sent waves throughout me
Of this caressing calm.
Then there came a whisper

Merging with ethereal accents
I instinctively absorbed
As I began to glow.
In a state of metamorphosis
From shade to shade
In shimmers of jade
A tinkering in transition.
Then I stood where she was
One of such beauty
A vision to behold
Twas love at first sight.

I Am

I am as is the wind
A breath of fresh air
Upon the currents
Reinvigorating life itself.
I am as is a rain shower
Cleansing with sheets of droplets
Purifying from above
To all that lies below.
With a forest's reliance
To see it flourish
In vibrant foliage
With a menagerie of hues.
I am as the sun
In its eternal warmth
Soothing to the spirit
Gushing in golden glows.
From tip to the root
Across all landscapes
From mountains with sharp peaks
To coasts with thundering waves.
I am as is a bee
Buzzing about its business
Pollenating plants
Creating sites of new birth.
I am as a painter
Splashing with intent
In ardent striations
In sparkling sprinkles.
A dash here, a pinch there

A smile with a tear
To capture the fullness
To enhance, not lessen.
I am as is the moon
In all of its shapes
In its shimmering splendour
Bringing replenishing tides.
I am as this humble earth
Enduring the spectrum
In spheres of atmospheres
In dimensions of delight.

Divide

As there are two sides
To any coin
Or to a story
The same applies,
To people or spirits
Being of the light
Or those from a hurtful nature
Depending on this divide,
Where one happens to reside
Those yet low functioning
Have this preoccupation
Fascination with evil concepts.
It takes all kinds
To make the world go around
But why do some ?
Find it so necessary,
To feed off of
The sadness of others
This is a below moral structure
The bottom of the barrel.
What most don't realize
Is that there will come a day
Be it sooner or later
When this pendulum,
Swings back and when it does
This person's misfortune
Although so deserved
Is not acted upon,
In the same manner

Due to this mercy
Which is an attribute
Of those with a conscience.
As this is accorded
So should it be returned
As a courtesy
Being part of an,
Elevated awareness
Elements to eschew
If we wish to ascend
For a loving heart is from a higher existence.

Wink and A Smile

Keep tapping your foot
To the beat of the music
Let your soul sing long
Even throughout your sleep.
Be of what you're made of
Be proud of this heritage
A privileged legacy
Whose lengths linger,
In an echoing tunnel
Spinning and turning
In a soft sereneness
In resonating decibals.
As you entered life in fine form
Humming a tune
That has kept its tempo
Those eyes are dancing,
As they go about
Their merry way
So darting here and there
In skipping motions.
Each has its own purpose
A lock and a key
That opens its petals
As you arise in morning.
Whose scents you inhale
Being the impetus
What is behind
What propels you forward.
As even in the rain

Do you make the most of it
You can change polarities
With a wink and a smile.
Your heart is its own violin
Like you float upon waters
Being lighter than air
Of a feathery wispiness.
So kick up your heels
Float on a stream
Absorb its misty spray
In reveling invigorations.

Branches Of Freedom

From tree to tree
One chases the other
But they're not of the same kind
Which makes this very strange,
Yet even more
It's the smaller blackbird
In pursuit of
The larger crow.
This makes a sight
Have a double take
To see if I have this right
Each night is repeated.
To see them darting about
Funny type of game
Up and down, then all around
Even skimming the ground.
They return without fail
Then perched on limbs
One above another
Screeching with flapping wings.
Once more off they go
Into the wild blue yonder
Continuing on
In their tradition.
A certain friendship
With its origins
In the branches of freedom
Where upon they found,
What has to this day

Been old reliable
From the crack of dawn
In their hearts both have shone.
The dynamic duo
With the ruffle of feathers
So announce their presence
Into the welcoming skies,
Which smile endlessly
Seeing what transpires
Two birds from opposite ends
Who share a common theme.

Stopover

The rustling of paper
The eerie feeling
I wasn't alone
That there was a presence.
Then there was silence
Could hear a pin drop
Just me and whatever
Was still, but not for long.
As within the hour
A door rattled
Out in the hall
All senses were then on high alert.
I was beside myself
I went through the scenarios
Of what this could be
I came to the conclusion.
That this was a spirit
So I asked it to leave
Saying it did not belong here
Yet a minute after,
I had finished
I received a text
On my cell phone
"This is where I live. "
Well that sure did it
To have confirmation
Showed me this was
Not your ordinary,
Run of the mill ghost

Yet I was adamant
No matter how persistent
This entity was,
That under no circumstance
Was this their final destination
This was merely
A stopover.
Then I heard footsteps
As a door swung open
With the last clang
So was made a grand departure.

Between Our Hearts

Are we too young ?
These feelings inside
Tell us otherwise
That as this unfolds,
We are right in the middle
Square in the center
Of a tug of war
Which is between our hearts.
Which side will prevail ?
Emotions or common sense
Do we throw caution ?
Into the wind.
As we are right in the middle
Square in the center
Of a tug of war
Which is between our hearts.
I pull you close to me
Find it hard to fight the urge
Like a geyser inside
This pushes up to the surface.
I look in your eyes
I hear the soft words
They take me where
To heights I've never known.
As we are right in the middle
Square in the center
Of a tug of war
Which is between our hearts.
So inch back and forth

The lines are drawn
It all comes down to
If this is real or not.
There is temptation
Do we give in or resist ?
We come to a point
Of no return.
As we are right in the middle
Square in the center
Of a tug of war
Which is between our hearts.

Same Language

A darting hawk
Flew in front of my truck
Had to catch my breath
Was such a fine omen,
Of what may transpire
As this was a sign
One that did not escape
Its importance or meaning.
For in a lifetime
You may be fortunate
To have one such
Magical occurrence.
Such a low frequency
Says you savour the moment
To the fullest degree
In its highest relevance.
So this did not fall
On deaf ears or blind eyes
All channels are open
To what may come next.
Then that same night
Did my spouse and myself
Observe a bright light
A meteorite in the sky.
Was there and then gone
In an instant
Like a ball of fire
On a vanishing descent.
Putting the two together

Are like these two book ends
That have so much to say
With what's written in between.
Each step taken
So leaves an imprint
As paths are crossed
So are memories etched,
With indelible marks
That do not stand alone
Are like trees in a forest
That speak the same language.

Right Mind

Try to get my head around this
Just don't understand
How a child is put in harm's way
Morals or a conscience,
Would put an end to that
But when one is without
Such basic scruples
They empower themselves.
To do the unthinkable
With checks and balances
An ounce of prevention
Walls are there to deter.
Yet tragic occurrences
Can and do happen
To the innocent
Due to an imperfect system.
Anger erupts
As in such blatant
Abuses of trust
A victim's eyes are tainted.
From a failure to protect
There is no explanation
Why one then can't sleep at night
From what they endured.
When they come forth
As a silence is broken
Hearts are shattered
By the magnitude,
Of the indignation

A damage that's done
As reality sets in
Tempers begin to flare.
Could not have seen it coming
What would possess ?
A person to perpetrate
Such a dastardly deed.
No one in their right mind
Is capable of
This heinous act
Then deprives one of the light in their soul.

Unparallelled Pronunciation

In the event
That a stone comes freely
Into my possession
I will welcome,
It openly
To nurture their existence
As well as my own
How two circles interconnect.
Two worlds form together
This common ground
For a time, in a space
Which creates these,
Positive vibrations
To have and to share
In an air of consensus
Where we know we need to be.
To benefit from
A quietness
In a sphere of
This auric metamorphosis.
To hear the birds sing
In this serene chorus
Which takes us to a haven
Where we walk placidly.
To bring those near
Who are destined
To enter this realm
With a raised awareness.
To be of a mindfulness

On a level plane
To communicate
When language is no barrier.
As restrictions are removed
All becomes possible
To reach with a belief
To stand as equal entities.
Not above or below
But side by side
To usher in an era
Of unparalleled pronunciation.

Adorning Adorations

The green in this field
Matches your inner glow
Like a stream whose ripples
Have an orchard,
Within their seams
So kick up your heels
Up and down the lane
Dancing to celtic rhythms.
In you are streaks
Sets the sky ablaze
With striking hues
Of adorning adorations.
As life is meant
To be taken in strides
Not all at once
In equal leaps,
The air beneath
Is your liberation
An expression of
The wisps that surround you.
Like little fairies
Whose wings tickle
With their feather tips
As your spirit takes flight.
To where it's destined
To a place beyond
These physical confines
In between lines of light.
You just go with

What's there in the moment
So adapt to the currents
As they race across,
Over hill and dale
Of which you are a part
An integral essence
As no one is an island.
You emulate yourself
We all breathe the same air
But it's how you go about this
So defines who you are.

Serene Contemplations

There you were alone
Sitting by a brook
So lovely and all
Singing a touching tune.
There I was walking by
Then as I stood
For I was transfixed
By this image,
Of your beauty
You then cast a smile
Which blessed this day
In a dazzling premonition.
That here in this midst
Was the origin of time
As we controlled the hands
To hold this moment still.
As your eyes met mine
A river did rejoice
As your sweet voice was heard
A soft echo began,
It was as if
This was known before
As when I awoke
That very morning,
I knew I'd be
Forever changed
By what was an enigma
When I saw you,
I came to my senses

For I was given
Unconditionally
A vision to caress.
As I held you in my arms
The earth found a warmth
A tender loving ray
Became ours to share.
We have an eternity
To explore the possibilities
Of an unbridled passion
In serene contemplations.

Dawning Horizons

Never lose sight of
What first got you here
Elbows to the grindstone
Humble ethic.
Be the person
Stick to what you know
Don't sell yourself short
Not on any count.
Take the high road
Don't lower your standards
Stay where you belong
Where you do your best work.
Keep your head above water
Don't sink to the bottom
Let the cream come
To an auspicious top.
Roll with the punches
Don't take life too personal
Absorb the waves
Without going under,
You can be your worst critic
Don't be too hard on yourself
Challenge to the highest
Be fearless to fall,
If you are down
Get right back up
Don't dwell on the negative
Accent resilience.
That which illuminates

Needs constant care
To ensure its embers
Stay lit for the duration.
Stoke your glowing orb
Let its glitter shine
Hold what's dear, close to your heart
With an unequalled love.
You have inside
All that's required
To make a difference
To elicit dawning horizons.

Time And Space

You go into a situation
Head first, not feet first
One just doesn't dive in
They scan their surroundings,
An act of self-preservation
Not to be blindsided
But to be cognizant
Of these dynamics.
As each has an impact
Upon the other
A domino effect
Why you don't want to slip,
Between the cracks
By being complacent
As your eyes and ears
Need to be attuned,
To have the instincts
Which are necessary
To avoid pitfalls
That can and do happen,
If your rear view mirror
Has distortion
For one reason
This leads to endangerment.
Such is the last thing
You want to be
Troubled about
Why add to the confusion ?
This is contrary

To what you wish for
So it only makes sense
To keep your slate clean.
By having good habits
You stay in front
Not getting lost behind
A runaway freight train.
So you think before
You begin to respond
As it's this time and space
Which gives the chance to manoeuvre.

Exposures

When you come up against
What's like a brick wall
Do you stiffen your resolve ?
Or do you back away.
Adversity builds character
It can be a nemesis
By the right attitude
This can work in your favour.
It is perception
You can turn what appears
To be the last stand
Into a strengthening hand.
You can literally
Conquer your fears
Or let them eat you alive
Each exists side by side.
If someone tells me
That I can't succeed
Who is the defeatist ?
If I accept such lies.
We each have our
Own life to lead
To do with as we please
To steer its rudder.
An opposing current
Is no reason to submit,
A learning experience
Prepares us for the next hurdle.
I don't want a

Walk in the park
This serves no purpose
Nor develops,
Any useful skills
For if the reservoir
Is empty and dry
When a desert presents itself,
We're up a creek
Without a paddle
My repertoire is full
From all of my exposures.

Ringing Resonations

You were musically inclined
Right from the get go
There was rhythm
In your flowing steps,
You made the transition
From what tones appeared
Dancing in your head
To beats you sounded,
On these tapping drums
You'd be in a forest
Going from tree to tree
Such life you brought,
To awaiting skies
For in you is this spirit
With exclamation
To reach the highest heights.
You live and breathe
With resolution
These vibrant lines
Jump forth from exuberance.
It is hard to keep
Your feet on the ground
They levitate
In waves of wavelengths.
Within these are notes
Attached to symbols
To circulate around
To touch those destined.
You raise the bar

To unknown realms
Creating decibels
In expanding proportions.
There is a light presence
In elevating rays
Which leave a person
Ascended from where you were.
That stays with them
In ringing resonations
By each succeeding one
So emerges new found hope.

Close Succession

To be by the ocean
With the rush of the waves
You stand in the shallows
So feel the pull,
From a thousand generations
As lives you pass through
One after the other
In close succession.
Start to reminisce
As these memories
Have not forgotten
From whence they came.
You go to places
Have left their mark
These ports of entry
Trigger flashbacks.
These magical moments
Are links in a chain
As you shift in the sand
So do you transcend.
From one story
Each ridge represents
In a smooth transition
In a seamless tunnel.
You could see yourself
In broad daylight
In a sequence
Of poignant images.
In a maturation process

Of relevance
In karma cognizance
You instinctively know,
Where to go and when
There is no guesswork
As you are your own
Kind of dowsing rod.
As the sun shimmers
On the sparkling waters
The clouds overhead
Speak to you of having heart.

Never Ends

Has it been that long ?
Sounds like an old song
That we have been friends
Story that never ends.
Way back in highschool
Colours of black and gold
So many rules
We were brave and bold.
Has it been that long?
Sounds like an old song
That we have been friends
Story that never ends.
How the years have passed
As if in the fast lane
With the foot on the gas
Through the sun and rain.
So we've remained
True to ourselves
Values engrained
Between us top shelf.
Has it been that long ?
Sounds like an old song
That we have been friends
Story that never ends.
So it's been written
To always withstand
The test of time by ten
With its immortal sands.
Has it been that long ?

Sounds like an old song
That we have been friends
Story that never ends.
Up and down the field
Honour with integrity
Courage that never yields
To any adversity.
Has it been that long ?
Sounds like an old song
That we have been friends
Story that never ends.

Shining Bend

For a dream to come true
Have to live and breathe
Not holding your breath
Waiting to hitch a ride.
You supply the energy
The initial motion
The inner motivation
To set the wheels turning.
Once they start to spin
It is a matter
Of constant upkeep
To realize what,
Is within your grasp
The difference
Is extraordinary
When you are on side,
With your wants on one hand
Then your will in the other
There is a synergy
So reacts in kind.
As you get a glimpse
A glimmer of
That which is around
A shining bend.
This then enhances
A shooting star phenomena
By the law of attraction
By equal forces,
Then working towards

This destination
The center of your galaxy
The heart of your destiny.
The connection between
So builds upon
Is reinforced
By consensus,
Derived through an insight
A vision of brilliance
So manifests itself
In the form of a physical presence.

Synthesis Of Sentience

The word is getting out
Through many wheels
Thoughts are being dispersed
To the universe.
For what comes to you
Are terms of relevance
So puts ideas
Into a perspective,
Where most can make sense
Of what may otherwise
Just be beyond
A normal comprehension.
You're like an interpreter
You have ways to explain
Where others find
Truth in these meanings.
So you unlock
These hidden treasures
By deciphering
Pages of text.
In so doing
You relay messages
As would an emissary
By transcribing,
Ascended languages
Of ancient script
For these are teachings
To elevate,
A consciousness

So lower echelons
Share a raised awareness
To rise to the occasion.
As we are nearing a mark
A time is soon upon
When we will enter
An enlightening dawn.
Under this auspicious orb
A synthesis of sentience
Will make itself known
Showering those destined with cerebral intuition.